View the Zoo A
Kids Book

Billy Grinslott & Kinsey Marie Books
ISBN 9781957881522
Copyright, all rights reserved

In the Amphibian section at the zoo, there are different frogs. Frogs have excellent night vision and are very sensitive to movement. Frogs were the first land animals with vocal cords we call it a croak. The Bull frog has a loud croak.

There are many turtles on display at the zoo. The most popular are the Galapagos turtles. They're the biggest tortoises in the world. They're also the oldest. They can live for a year without food or water. They like taking naps.

There are different types of snakes at the zoo. The Boa Constrictor is one of the popular ones. They get their name because they wrap themselves around things. They have a lot of strength when they wrap themselves around something and can crush it. It's best not to let a boa constrictor wrap around you, because they can hurt you.

The anaconda is another popular snake. Anacondas are the world's largest snake. It can grow up to 30 feet long, about as long as your school bus. A full-grown anaconda can weigh up to 550 pounds. Anacondas are constrictors. They kill their prey by squeezing it to death just like a boa constrictor.

The rattlesnake got its name because it can make a rattling noise with its tail. It shakes it tail to warn you that you are too close, and you need to leave. Rattlesnakes are the largest venomous snakes in the United States. As with all snakes, if you see in the wild, you should leave immediately and don't bother them. They will bite and their venom is very poisonous.

You will see many reptiles at the zoo. Some of them include the lizard family like Iguanas, Gila monsters and many more of the lizard family. Lizards come in all sizes and colors and are cool to look at.

Beavers have a flat tail they use to slap on the water when they are frightened. Beavers like to chew down trees and build dams that they can live in. Beavers are powerful swimmers that can swim underwater for up to 15 minutes.

Some other critters you might see at the zoo are otters. Otters have the thickest fur of any animal. Otters are clever creatures, they'll use rocks to crack open the clams. Some Otters snuggle and hold hands while they are sleeping.

Pee-ewe what is that stinky critter with the big bushy tail. It smells bad. Skunks are normally curious and friendly unless you scare them. If you scare them, they will flip their bushy tale at you and spray you with a smelly potion and it stinks.

Some other critters you may see at the zoo, are Weasels and Ferrets. The black footed ferret is most common. Many people have had ferrets as pets for a long time. Ferrets are very smart and can even solve problems. Ferrets are smarter than cats and dogs.

There will be members of the dog family at many zoos. Like foxes, coyotes, and wolves, this is a red fox. Foxes are very vocal and make 40 different sounds. Foxes have impeccable hearing. Foxes are extremely playful.

The wolf is one of the biggest members of the dog family. They have a loud howl that sends chills down your spine. The timber wolf is the biggest of all the wolves. Pups are born deaf and blind with bright blue eyes until they mature.

Flamingos get their color from their food. Flamingos are filter feeders and turn their heads upside down to eat. A group of flamingos is called a flamboyance.

You may see owls at the zoo. The great horned owl is named for the tufts of feathers that sit atop its head. Great Horned Owls aren't all the same color. They mostly come out at night. They have a hoo-h'HOO-hoo-hoo, call that is unique and very recognizable.

Quack, Quack, Quack. What are those birds that are floating on the water? They are ducks. There are many different kinds of ducks at the zoo, these are Mallards. Ducks can float and have webbed feet to help them swim. Their feathers repel water, so they don't get wet. Baby ducks are called ducklings, a male duck is a drake, and a female duck is a hen.

The ostrich has the longest legs and neck of any bird species. Ostriches can't fly even though they have wings. They run instead of flying. With their long legs they can run up to 45 miles per hour. Ostrich's legs are strong, and they can front kick other animals. Ostriches live in small flocks and check their eggs by sticking their head into the hole where their eggs are. Ostriches like water and enjoy taking baths.

Puffins, nicknamed sea parrots or clowns of the see. Because their big orange beak looks like a parrots or clown's nose. A puffin's beak changes color during the year. In spring it blooms with an outrageous orange color. When flying, Puffins flap their wings up to 400 times a minute and fly up to 55 mph.

You will see different types of birds of prey at the zoo, like hawks, falcons, and eagles. Bald Eagles are very adaptive and live in just about every part of the world including the arctic regions. The bald eagle is America's national bird. The bald eagle gets their name due to their white hair on their head.

The Roseate spoonbill got its name because of its pink color and its beak is shaped like a big spoon. They use their spoon shaped beak to take big gulps of water that have food in them. When it walks, the roseate spoonbill swings its head back and forth in a sideways motion. The Roseate Spoonbill is 1 of 6 species of spoonbills in the world and the only one found in America.

There are many different types of birds at the zoo. There will be domestic and tropical birds. The most common ones are Parrots, eagles, ducks, peacock's, falcons, owls, cranes, pelicans, toucans, ostriches, and emus.

Orangutans are the biggest and heaviest tree-dwelling animal. They've got long arms. They eat with their feet. They build nests to sleep in. Some orangutans use sticks and rocks as tools.

The sloth gets its name because it moves really slow. Sloths move so slowly that algae and fungi have time to land and grow on them. Sloths are blind. They are faster in water than on land. It takes sloths 30 days to digest their food because their metabolism is so slow. They are 3 times stronger than humans.

There are many monkeys and chimpanzees at the zoo. The most popular is the spider monkey. Spider monkeys have strong tails and can hang from them. They Don't Have Thumbs like other monkeys. They are swinging specialists. They are social animals and like to hang out in groups.

Gorillas have hands and feet like humans including thumbs and big toes. Some gorillas in captivity have learned to use sign language to communicate with humans. Gorillas pound their chest as a type of communication. People share around 98% of our DNA with gorillas. They are one of the biggest, most powerful living primates. They have 16 different types of calls. Gorillas live in small groups called troops or bands.

Caribou are also known as reindeer. Reindeer are covered in hair from their nose to the bottom of their hooves. Reindeer are the only deer species to be widely domesticated.

Kudus are the largest member of the antelope family. They have cool looking spiral horns. They prefer warmer climates so you may see them is a southern zoo. Only 16 zoos across the U.S. display the kudu.

There may some types of deer at the zoo. The whitetail deer is the most popular deer in North America. A male deer is called a buck, a female is a doe, and a baby is called a fawn. Whitetail deer have good eyesight and hearing. Many zoos will let you feed corn to the deer.

Some zoos will have Guanaco, Alpacas or Llamas. Llamas are excellent guardians. Llamas have sharp eyes and ears and are quite intelligent. Llamas are known for spitting at other animals and even humans. So be careful when approaching one, it may spit at you.

There are many sheep at the zoo, this is a Dall sheep. The body of Dall sheep is covered with a white woolly coat that provides protection against low temperatures. Both males and females have horns. The age of the sheep can be calculated from the number of growth rings on their horns.

Some zoos will have Bison or Buffalos, this is a Bison. Bison and Buffalo sometimes are confused as the same animal. Buffalos have short hair. Bison have long hair on their back, front legs, and face. They also have a long beard. Bison are one of the strongest and largest animals on the planet.

Some zoos will have penguins you can see. Even though penguins have what looks like wings, they are actually flippers they use to swim with. The emperor penguin is the largest penguin. Penguins like to huddle together when its cold out. They also like sliding in the snow. Penguins are excellent swimmers and divers.

The Polar Bear is the biggest bear on earth. Male polar bears can weigh up to 1500 lbs. They like swimming and can swim constantly for days at a time. Polar bears keep warm thanks to the blubber under their skin. They can smell up to a mile away. They can run 25 mph and swim up to 10mph.

You might see an alligator at the zoo. Alligators are very social reptiles and prefer to live in groups called congregation. They are excellent and fast swimmers. Alligators are reptiles. Alligators will eat just about anything.

In the water world at the zoo, you can see seals, different types of fish and other creatures. But the most fun one to watch are the dolphins. They are very playful, and many zookeepers can train them to do tricks. Some dolphins will fetch a ball like a dog does. They are fun to watch.

Many zoos exhibit seals. The smallest seal is the Galapagos seal the largest is the elephant seal. Seals can sleep underwater. Seals can be hooligans, they like to have fun and are very friendly. Mother seals and pups bond with a unique call.

Sea Lions and seals like to have fun. Many zookeepers train sea lions and seals to fetch balls and other toys. Sea lions and seals are very social and can be taught tricks. They like to play and have fun.

Many zoos will have bears on exhibit. Not only can you see a polar bear, but some zoos have black bears, brown bears or grizzly bears. Brown bears are the most widely spread bear across America. Bears can climb trees. Bears have excellent senses of smell, sight, and hearing. They can actually see in colors like you can.

Zebras are part of the horse family. New born foals, baby zebras can stand after 6 minutes. Baby zebras have brown stripes when they are born and as they mature, they turn black. A herd or group of zebras is called a dazzle.

What are those animals with long legs and necks? They are Giraffes. They are the tallest mammal on earth. Their long legs and neck help them to eat leaves from the trees. New-born baby giraffes are taller than most humans and they can stand within 30 minutes. Giraffes can sleep standing up like a horse. Giraffes are super peaceful animals. They are easy to get along with.

Elephants are the largest land animal. They have huge ears. They can grab stuff with their trunks. Elephants eat all day long. They can't jump like other animals and humans. Elephants communicate with vibrations in the ground. Baby elephants can stand within 20 minutes after birth. Elephants are very smart. They never forget anything. Elephants purr like cats as a form of communication.

There are many cats at the zoo. In the northern zoos may have a snow leopard. Other zoos may have bobcats. These cats are used to living in colder climates. They can't roar like other big cats. They wrap their tail around their head and neck and use it as a scarf for warmth. Their paws are huge and make good snowshoes for traveling in the snow.

Some of the other cats that zoos have are black panthers, bobcats, and cougars, otherwise known as mountain lions. Mountain lions, pumas, and cougars are all the same species. Mountain lions are the biggest of these cats and live just about everywhere in America.

Tigers are considered one of the most beautiful cats by many, because of their astonishing looks and black stripes. Tigers are the largest amongst all the wild cats. They are strong and can knock things down with one swipe of their paw. Tiger cubs are born blind until their eyes develop. Tigers live for 25 years, and they love to swim and play in the water.

These are lions. They are known as the king of the jungle because of their raw power and strength. Lions don't fear other animals. The roar of a lion can be heard 5 miles away. Lions like to live in groups known as a pride. Male lions have mains and females do not. Female lions gather most of the food and male lions protect the herd and the young cubs, baby lions.

Fun Facts About Zoos

Some states have free zoos that you can visit.

Over 600 million people visit zoos each year.

There are 2,800 zoos & aquariums in the world.

The United States has at least 355 zoos.

The oldest zoo in the world is Vienna Zoo.

The Philadelphia zoo is the oldest in the USA.

There are different animals at each zoo.

Zoos and Aquariums protect endangered species.

Zoos and Aquariums rehabilitate injured animals.

You can see animals that you may never get to see.

Author Page

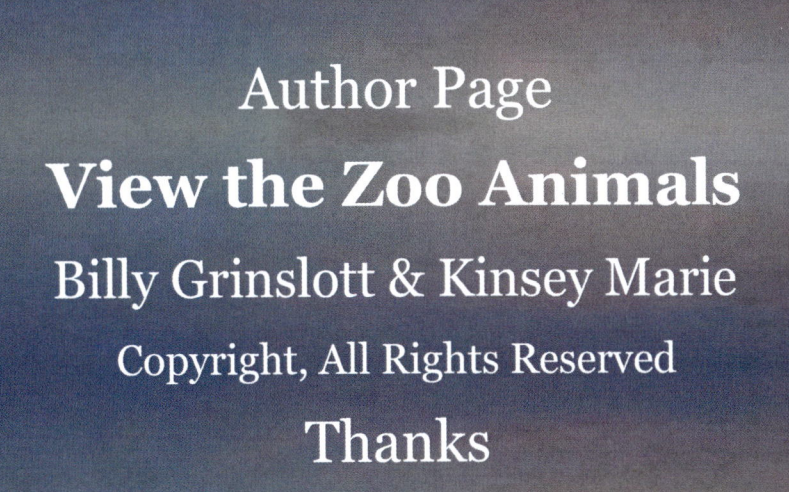

View the Zoo Animals

Billy Grinslott & Kinsey Marie

Copyright, All Rights Reserved

Thanks

ISBN 978-1957881522

To Check Out More Our Kids Books.

Visit Kinsey Marie Books or Billy Grinslott